Join my facebook coloring group and get a lot of free coloring books and coloring pages

IMPRESSUM / IMPRINT
Monsoon Publishing LLC
Email: info@monsoonpublishing.de
www.monsoonpublishing.de
facebook.com/monsoonpublishingllc

Monsoon Publishing LLC
www.monsoonpublishing.com
info@monsoonpublishing.com
facebook.com/monsoonpublishingusa

www.ingramcontent.com/pod-product-compliance
Ingram Content Group UK Ltd.
Pitfield, Milton Keynes, MK11 3LW, UK
UKHW051302121225
9545UKWH00048B/858

9 783758 409448